EXPLORING COUNTRIES

The Netherlands

by Lisa Owings

Note to Librarians, Teachers, and Parents:

Blastoff! Readers are carefully developed by literacy experts and combine standards-based content with developmentally appropriate text.

Level 1 provides the most support through repetition of high-frequency words, light text, predictable sentence patterns, and strong visual support.

Level 2 offers early readers a bit more challenge through varied simple sentences, increased text load, and less repetition of high-frequency words.

Level 3 advances early-fluent readers toward fluency through increased text and concept load, less reliance on visuals, longer sentences, and more literary language.

Level 4 builds reading stamina by providing more text per page, increased use of punctuation, greater variation in sentence patterns, and increasingly challenging vocabulary.

Level 5 encourages children to move from "learning to read" to "reading to learn" by providing even more text, varied writing styles, and less familiar topics.

Whichever book is right for your reader, Blastoff! Readers are the perfect books to build confidence and encourage a love of reading that will last a lifetime!

This edition first published in 2013 by Bellwether Media, Inc.

No part of this publication may be reproduced in whole or in part without written permission of the publisher. For information regarding permission, write to Bellwether Media, Inc., Attention: Permissions Department, 5357 Penn Avenue South, Minneapolis, MN 55419.

Library of Congress Cataloging-in-Publication Data
Owings, Lisa.
The Netherlands / by Lisa Owings.
   p. cm. – (Blastoff! Readers–exploring countries)
Includes bibliographical references and index.
Summary: "Developed by literacy experts for students in grades three through seven, this book introduces young readers to the geography and culture of the Netherlands"–Provided by publisher.
ISBN 978-1-60014-766-1 (hardcover : alk. paper)
1. Netherlands–Juvenile literature. I. Title.
DJ18.O95 2013
949.2–dc23   2012003337

Printed in the United States of America, North Mankato, MN.

Contents

Where Is the Netherlands? 4
The Land 6
Polders 8
Wildlife 10
The People 12
Daily Life 14
Going to School 16
Working 18
Playing 20
Food 22
Holidays 24
Tulip Mania 26
Fast Facts 28
Glossary 30
To Learn More 31
Index 32

Where Is the Netherlands?

Did you know?

The people of the Netherlands are called Dutch. About four out of every ten Dutch people live in the Holland region.

North Sea

N
W   E
S

★
Amsterdam

Netherlands

Belgium

fun fact

Netherlands means "low-lying country." More than a quarter of the land is lower than the level of the sea.

Germany

The Netherlands is a country in northwestern Europe covering 16,040 square miles (41,543 square kilometers). It borders Belgium to the south and Germany to the east. Much of the Netherlands touches water. The North Sea crashes against its northern and western shores. Rivers and **canals** crisscross the country.

The Netherlands is divided into 12 **provinces**. The region of Holland includes the provinces of North Holland and South Holland. Amsterdam in North Holland is the country's capital and largest city. Many people still call the Netherlands *Holland* because of the important cities in the region.

Did you know?

The West Frisian Islands form a chain off the Netherlands' northern coast. Their sandy beaches make them popular vacation spots for the Dutch as well as tourists.

The Netherlands is known for its flat land. **Dunes** and **dikes** push back the North Sea. Behind these barriers, green farmland covers much of the country. Many fields are full of bright flowers in spring.

Lakes sparkle in the northwestern Netherlands. IJsselmeer is the largest lake. It was formed by a **dam**. The Rhine, Maas, and Schelde Rivers all meander through the Netherlands and into the North Sea. Land rises in the southeast, where forests spread across gently sloping hills.

fun fact

It rains so much in the Netherlands that many Dutch carry a raincoat or umbrella wherever they go.

IJsselmeer

Did you know?

After a deadly flood in 1953, the Dutch built dams and strengthened dikes throughout the country. Today they direct floodwaters to safe places instead of trying to hold them back.

Around 2,500 square miles (6,475 square kilometers) of the Netherlands used to be underwater. The Dutch built dikes offshore to hold back the sea. Then they used **windmills** to pump out the water behind the dikes. These drained areas are called polders.

Polders are flat and tidy landscapes. Canals run through rectangular plots of farmland. Windmills and cows are common sights. Many of the Netherlands' major cities were built on polders. Flooding is a constant danger on this type of land.

red
deer

The Dutch share their land with a variety of animals.
Muddy **wetlands** between the islands and the
mainland are a paradise for birdwatchers. Flocks of
black storks, purple herons, and Eurasian spoonbills stop
for a meal or spend the winter. Oystercatchers use their
long beaks to dig **shellfish** out of the sand.

Eurasian spoonbill

red fox

Arctic tern

fun fact

The rare Arctic tern sometimes comes to the West Frisian Islands to raise its young before it heads toward the South Pole. It travels farther each year than any other bird.

Deer and wild boars wander through Hoge Veluwe National Park. Foxes, badgers, and polecats also live in protected forests. Lakes and rivers hold fish, frogs, and water snakes. The **endangered** pond bat swoops above the water and plucks insects out of the night sky.

Did you know?

People in the province of Friesland speak Frisian, the Netherlands' second official language.

The Netherlands is home to nearly 17 million people. About eight out of every ten people have Dutch **ancestors**. The country is also home to many **immigrants**. Most are from other European countries. Others came from Indonesia, Turkey, Morocco, and Suriname. Dutch is the most widely spoken language.

The Dutch are known for accepting beliefs and ways of life that are different from their own. They have a long history of welcoming those who were rejected elsewhere because of their religious or **political** beliefs. However, the Dutch government has adopted stricter requirements for the country's immigrants.

Speak Dutch!

English	Dutch	How to say it
hello	hallo	HAH-loh
good-bye	tot ziens	TOTE ZEENS
yes	ja	yah
no	nee	nay
please	alstublieft	AHLS-too-bleeft
thank you	dank u	DAHNGK oo
friend (male)	vriend	vreent
friend (female)	vriendin	vrihn-DIHN

Did you know?
Most Dutch homes do not have curtains covering the windows. It is not unusual for strangers to peer inside as they walk past.

More than eight out of every ten Dutch people live in cities. Most live in and around Amsterdam, Rotterdam, and The Hague. Buses and trains make it easy for people to get around these large cities. However, many Dutch prefer to ride their bicycles. Most return to cozy apartments or townhouses at the end of the day.

Those who live in the countryside are usually close to a city or town. They often shop and chat with friends at local outdoor markets. Many families in the countryside rise early to work on their farms. In a few small villages, people still wear wooden shoes and **traditional** clothing.

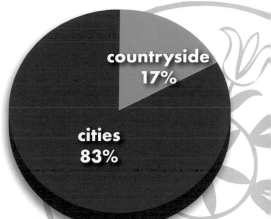

Where People Live in the Netherlands

countryside
17%

cities
83%

Children in the Netherlands begin school at age 4 or 5. Elementary school lasts until age 12. Students take math, social studies, Dutch, art, and gym classes. Children in the province of Friesland also learn the Frisian language.

Dutch students can choose one of three types of high schools. One type trains students for specific jobs. Another prepares them for **professional school**. The final option is for students who plan to attend a university. Choosing a high school can be difficult for Dutch students. Teachers and test results help them make this important decision.

Did you know?

Artists in Delft paint beautiful designs on pottery that is famous worldwide. Others still make traditional wooden shoes, metal dishes, and fancy clocks.

About eight out of every ten workers in the Netherlands have **service jobs**. They help run the country's businesses, schools, and hospitals. They also work in restaurants, hotels, and shops that serve both locals and **tourists**. Factory workers produce fuel, electronics, and other **exports**.

Most of the countryside is used for farming. Dutch farmers raise cows for milk, butter, and cheese. They also grow colorful vegetables and flowers. Offshore, fishers cast their nets for herring, **mussels**, and shrimp.

Where People Work in the Netherlands

services 80%

manufacturing 18%

farming 2%

Did you know?
In the Frisian sport of fierljeppen, people use tall poles to leap over canals.

fierljeppen

The Dutch like to be outdoors year-round. Spring is the perfect time for cycling, soccer, and tennis. In summer, the country's beaches are packed with swimmers. Hikers enjoy the colors of tree-covered hills in fall, and ice-skating is a favorite winter activity.

On rainy days, many Dutch people stay home and curl up with a book. Others seek out a cozy café and a cup of coffee or hot chocolate. Some grab an umbrella and head to the nearest history or art museum. In the evenings, many Dutch go to concerts or plays.

fun fact

During the coldest winters, Dutch ice-skaters race over frozen canals. The most popular race winds 125 miles (200 kilometers) through 11 cities in Friesland.

Did you know?

The Netherlands is famous for its cheeses, especially Gouda and Edam. These cheeses end up on tables across the globe.

The Dutch enjoy rich, filling foods. For breakfast, most eat buttered bread. They top it with jam, cheese, or chocolate sprinkles. Market stalls sell fresh herring in the spring. Raw herring sandwiches are a favorite lunchtime snack. *Pannekoeken* are popular treats. These large pancakes are filled with fruit, cheese, or bacon. Fluffy *poffertjes* are smaller cakes sprinkled with sugar.

Dinner is the largest meal of the day. Many Dutch enjoy *hutspot*, a dish of potatoes, carrots, and onions. Smoked sausage often completes the meal. A thick pea soup called *snert* is a traditional winter dish served with rye bread.

poffertjes

snert

fun fact

The Netherlands consumes more licorice than any other nation in the world. Some Dutch licorice is salty rather than sweet.

Queen's Day

Dutch people look forward to both religious and national holidays. Fireworks crack, Christmas trees go up in flames, and people dive into the freezing sea to greet the New Year. During *Carnival* in spring, the streets fill with music and giant floats. The Dutch honor their queen by wearing orange on April 30, Queen's Day.

Sinterklaas is a favorite holiday for Dutch children. On December 5, they set out shoes for Saint Nicholas, or *Sinterklaas*. They fill the shoes with hay and carrots for his white horse. The next day, the shoes are full of gifts. Christmas celebrations take place on December 25 and 26. These two days are marked by feasts and family activities.

Sinterklaas

> **! fun fact**
>
> In the 1600s, the Dutch brought the *Sinterklaas* tradition with them to New York City. This inspired the North American tradition of Santa Claus.

Tulip Mania

Keukenhof Gardens

Did you know?

At the height of *tulipomania*, a single rare tulip could cost as much as a house!

The Netherlands has been wild about tulips for centuries. In the 1600s, the Dutch fell in love with the tulip's variety of colors and shapes. The flower became a popular symbol of wealth. By the 1630s, the Dutch were buying and selling tulips for large fortunes. This *tulipomania* ended in 1637 when prices stopped rising. Everyone tried to sell their tulips, but no one would buy them.

fun fact

Semper augustus was at one time the rarest and most desired type of tulip in the Netherlands. People later discovered that its beautiful pattern of red and white stripes was caused by a virus.

Today, the Dutch still grow most of the tulips sold worldwide. In spring, billions of tulips bloom throughout the country. Dazzling displays are planted each year in the Keukenhof Gardens, the largest flower garden in the world. The tulip has become a symbol of the beauty and international importance of the Netherlands.

Fast Facts About the Netherlands

The Netherlands' Flag

The flag of the Netherlands has three horizontal stripes. The top stripe is red, the middle white, and the bottom blue. The red stripe used to be orange in honor of the Prince of Orange, who helped the Dutch gain independence from Spain. However, the color orange was too faint in battle. The current flag was made official in 1937.

Official Name: Kingdom of the Netherlands

Area: 16,040 square miles
(41,543 square kilometers);
the Netherlands is the 135th
largest country in the world.

Capital City:	Amsterdam
Important Cities:	Rotterdam, The Hague, Utrecht, Leiden, Haarlem
Population:	16,730,632 (July 2012)
Official Languages:	Dutch, Frisian
National Holiday:	Queen's Day (April 30)
Religions:	Christian (50%), None (42%), Muslim (5.8%), Other (2.2%)
Major Industries:	construction, farming, fishing, fuel processing, manufacturing, services
Natural Resources:	natural gas, oil, peat, limestone, salt, sand, farmland
Manufactured Products:	fuel, electronics, chemicals, metals, food products
Farm Products:	dairy products, grains, cucumbers, potatoes, tomatoes, sugar beets, peppers, flowers
Unit of Money:	Euro; the euro is divided into 100 cents.

Glossary

ancestors—relatives who lived long ago

canals—artificial rivers that help control the flow of water; canals are often used to transport goods.

dam—a barrier across a stream or river that holds back water

dikes—high walls or barriers built to hold back water and prevent flooding

dunes—hills of sand formed by wind or water

endangered—at risk of becoming extinct

exports—products that a country sells to other countries

immigrants—people who leave one country to live in another country

mussels—shellfish that look similar to clams but have dark shells

political—relating to systems of government and power

professional school—a type of college that prepares students for careers in specific fields such as business, education, or healthcare

provinces—districts or regions within a country; provinces follow all the laws of the country and make some of their own laws.

service jobs—jobs that perform tasks for people or businesses

shellfish—small animals that live in water and have shells; oysters, clams, and mussels are shellfish.

tourists—people who are visiting a country

traditional—relating to stories, beliefs, or ways of life that families or groups hand down from one generation to the next

wetlands—wet, spongy land; bogs, marshes, and swamps are wetlands.

windmills—structures with long, rotating blades; windmills use wind power to grind grains and pump water.

To Learn More

AT THE LIBRARY

DiPiazza, Francesca. *Netherlands in Pictures.* Minneapolis, Minn.: Twenty-First Century Books, 2011.

Dodge, Mary Mapes. *Hans Brinker or The Silver Skates.* New York, N.Y.: Cosimo, 2005.

Noyes, Deborah. *Hana in the Time of the Tulips.* Cambridge, Mass.: Candlewick Press, 2004.

ON THE WEB

Learning more about the Netherlands is as easy as 1, 2, 3.

1. Go to www.factsurfer.com.

2. Enter "the Netherlands" into the search box.

3. Click the "Surf" button and you will see a list of related Web sites.

With factsurfer.com, finding more information is just a click away.

Index

activities, 20, 21
Amsterdam, 4, 5, 14
canals, 5, 9, 20, 21
capital (see Amsterdam)
Carnival, 24
daily life, 14-15
Delft, 18
dikes, 6, 8
education, 16-17
flooding, 8, 9
food, 22-23
Friesland, 12, 16, 21
The Hague, 14
holidays, 24-25
Holland, 4, 5
housing, 14
IJsselmeer, 7
immigration, 13
Keukenhof Gardens, 26, 27
landscape, 6-9
languages, 12, 13, 16
location, 4-5
people, 4, 12-13
polders, 8-9
Queen's Day, 24
Rotterdam, 14
Sinterklaas, 24, 25
sports, 20, 21
transportation, 14
Tulip Mania, 26-27

West Frisian Islands, 6, 11
wildlife, 10-11
windmills, 8, 9
working, 18-19